Reading Group Choices

*Selections for Lively
Book Discussions*

Paz & Associates

1997

For further information, contact:
Reading Group Choices
Paz & Associates
2106 Twentieth Avenue South
Nashville, TN 37212-4312

800/260-8605 — phone
615/298-9864 — fax
dpaz@pazbookbiz.com — e-mail

ISBN 0-9644876-2-4

Cover design by:
Mary Mazer
Art That Works
1651 Grove Street
San Diego, CA 92102
619/702-6041

Printed by:
Rich Printing Company, Inc.
7131 Centennial Bl.
Nashville, TN 37209
615/350-7300

*A portion of the proceeds from this publication will be
used to support literacy efforts throughout the United States.*

This publication is dedicated to the authors, agents, publishers, book distributors, and booksellers who bring us books that enrich our lives.

ACKNOWLEDGMENTS

This third edition of *Reading Group Choices* was inspired by the many readers who called, wrote and faxed us words of encouragement and appreciation for our first two editions. Even in these times of high technology, it's clear that reading is alive and well.

We wish to thank participating publishers for their support. This publication was made possible by their financial assistance, and their recognition of the importance of reading discussion groups. Our thanks to: Algonquin Books of Chapel Hill; Back Bay Books (Little, Brown & Co.); Chicory Blue Press; Chronicle Books; Conari Press; Counterpoint; Crown (Random House); Duke University Press; East/West Bridge Publishing House; Grosset/Putnam; Harmony Books (Random House); Hungry Mind Press; Alfred A. Knopf (Random House); Orlando Place Press; Papier-Mache Press; Pennsylvania State University Press; Riverhead Books (Putnam Publishing Group); Soho Press; Spinsters Ink; Sta-Kris, Inc.; Nan A. Talese (Bantam Doubleday Dell); Jeremy P. Tarcher, Inc. (Putnam Publishing Group); University of Missouri Press; Villard Books (Random House); and Vintage Books (Random House).

A special thanks to our Advisory Board of readers, reading discussion group leaders, and booksellers who shared their expertise and love of books to screen recommendations: Jean Bolinger, *Book Nook, Inc.*, Warren, Ohio; Trish Coffey, *Wellington's Books*, Cary, North Carolina; Maria C. Durbin, *Rainbow Books & Records*, Newark, Delaware; Rachel Jacobsohn, *Association of Book Group Readers & Leaders*, Highland Park, Illinois; Donna Lee Jonté, Associate Editor, *Belles Lettres: A Review of Books by Women*, University Park, Maryland; Kathy Schultenover, Book Club Coordinator, *Davis-Kidd Booksellers*, Nashville, Tennessee; Rick Smith; *Brodsky Bookshop*, Taos, New Mexico; and Susannah Vazehgoo, *The Concord Bookshop*, Concord, Massachusetts. To our readers, who developed discussion topics, we thank Megan DuBois, Barbara Richards Haugen, Pat Lane, Karen Stidham, and Del Tinsley.

For providing their technical expertise and affordable services, we thank Mary Mazer of Art That Works for her cover design, and John Craig and Tom Hutchins of Rich Printing Company, quality book printers since 1892.

And to Mark Kaufman, our editor and production manager, for sharing his many gifts and making these three editions possible.

INTRODUCTION

Every year, the process of putting together another selection of "discussible" books seems to grow more interesting. New small presses, previously unexplored topics, debut authors, compelling stories, and emerging social issues provide the kind of reading that helps us live and experience the world more deeply. Books can have such a profound influence on us.

In this edition of *Reading Group Choices,* you'll discover a number of titles that prompt us to think about matters of race and ethnicity — challenging our assumptions and helping us see with new perspective. Read about a black woman with white skin in *Notes of a White Black Woman,* then compare with the life of a black son of a white woman in *The Color of Water.* Experience the world of Julia Alvarez' Latina novelist Yolanda Garcia (introduced in her award-winning novel *How the Garcia Girls Lost Their Accents*) in *¡Yo!* through the stories her sisters and her third husband can hardly wait to tell.

In several other books, we learn about how some people have chosen to find spiritual meaning and a sense of place when life seems to grow increasingly complex and hectic. Kathleen Norris finds sanctuary within a Benedictine monastery in *The Cloister Walk.* Richard Louv's work *The Web of Life* has been described as "a quiet book in a noisy world." Where do we find a sense of community? In Mark Gerzon's *A House Divided,* we learn about six belief systems in America and what it will take for us to develop bridges to common ground. Is there any common ground to be found?

Some of our favorite authors return with new works. In *Alias Grace,* Margaret Atwood guides us into the complex mind of Grace Marks, an enigmatic criminal in the 1800s convicted of murder at the age of sixteen. Michael Crichton's *Airframe* puts the issue of airline safety into the public mind. Mary Pipher's last book, *Reviving Ophelia,* explored our culture's effects on the mental health of teenage girls; in *The Shelter of Each Other,* she addresses how we can reconnect with the healing strength that is present within all families.

Books by newly discovered authors show the richness that exists beyond the bestsellers. Veronica Chambers probes a daughter's journey of self-discovery, understanding, and forgiveness in *Mama's Girl.* Dawn Turner Trice, in *Only Twice I've Wished for Heaven,* pulls us into the life of 11-year-old Tempestt, who is drawn to the world outside her home and into the surrounding Chicago ghetto. Rochelle Hollander Schwab probes the complexity of the word "family" over custody battles and homosexual lifestyle issues in her new novel, *In A Family Way.*

Reading can take us to new worlds of understanding and help us sort the issues that surround us. We hope you enjoy choosing books from this diverse selection — and are enriched by the discussions that result from your reading.

Donna Paz
Nashville, Tennessee
January, 1997

CONTENTS

CONTENTS (continued)

CONTENTS (continued)

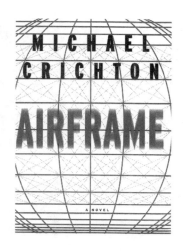

AIRFRAME

Author: Michael Crichton

Publisher: Alfred A. Knopf, 1996

Available in:
Hardcover, 352 pages. $26.00
(ISBN 0-679-44648-6)

Genre: Fiction

Summary

Three passengers are dead. Fifty-six are injured. The interior cabin virtually destroyed. But the pilot manages to land the plane ...

At a moment when the issue of safety and death in the skies is paramount in the public mind, a lethal mid-air disaster aboard a commercial twin-jet airliner bound from Hong Kong to Denver triggers a pressured and frantic investigation.

Airframe is nonstop reading: the extraordinary mixture of super suspense and authentic information on a subject of compelling interest that has been a Crichton hallmark since *The Andromeda Strain.*

Recommended by: Elizabeth Teachout, *Philadelphia Inquirer*

"A one-sitting read that will cause a lifetime of white-knuckled nightmares ... Much more scintillating than your typical disaster novel."

Author Biography

Michael Crichton was born in Chicago, in 1942. His novels include *The Andromeda Strain, The Great Train Robbery, Congo, Jurassic Park, Rising Sun,* and *Disclosure.* He is also the creator of the television series *ER.*

Topics to Consider

1 In addition to a dramatic story, Crichton also presents a wealth of technical information. Do you find these details interesting or distracting? Do they enhance the story?

2 Which individuals act responsibly and which irresponsibly? Does any institution fill the role of the "bad guy"?

3 What position does Crichton take on airline regulation, economic competition among the airlines, and the FAA?

4 What are the various attitudes toward the accident and what are the various motivations for seeking an explanation?

5 When the actual causes of the incident are discovered, why are they not made public?

6 We all like to think disasters won't happen to us. What factors in Crichton's scenario would allow you to say "this could never happen to me?"

7 Assuming the scenario in the book to be accurate, how is your image of airline safety affected?

8 Does this story have any moral? Crichton provides an epilogue of character updates and an accident report. Can you draw any ethical conclusions from these addenda?

ALIAS GRACE

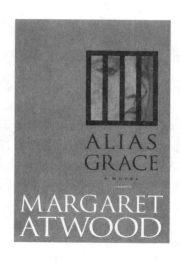

Author: Margaret Atwood

Publisher: Nan A. Talese/
Doubleday, 1996

Available in:
Hardcover, 468 pages. $24.95
(ISBN 0-385-47571-3)

Genre: Fiction

Summary

With details taken from original court documents, Atwood guides us into the complex mind of Grace Marks, one of the most "celebrated" and enigmatic criminals of the 1800s, convicted of a double murder at the age of sixteen. Grace herself has no recollection of the murders — for which she spent twenty-nine years in prison and fifteen months in a lunatic asylum — until the young Dr. Jordan, an early enthusiast of psychoanalysis, arrives to extract the details of the crime from her memory. Atwood leaves us to answer the question she herself still asks: "Was Grace Marks the cunning female demon many considered her to be, or was she simply a terrorized victim?"

Recommended by: *Maclean's*

"Brilliantly realized, intellectually provocative and maddeningly suspenseful ..."

Author Biography

Margaret Atwood is the author of more than twenty-five books. Her most recent works are the novels *The Robber Bride* and *Cat's Eye,* the story collections *Wilderness Tips* and *Good Bones and Simple Murders,* and a volume of poetry, *Morning in the Burned House.* Among the many honors she has received are the Canadian Governor General's Award, *The Sunday Times* Award for Literary Excellence in the U.K., and Le Chevalier dans l'Ordre des Arts et des Lettres in France. She lives in Toronto with the novelist Graeme Gibson.

Topics to Consider

1 The daily and seasonal rhythm of household work is described in detail. Compared to your own routines, how much has changed over the past one hundred years?

2 Atwood employs two main points of view and voices in the novel. Did you trust one more than the other? As the story progresses, does Grace's voice (in dialogue) in Simon's part of the story change? If yes, how and why?

3 Discuss the importance and use of dreams in the novel.

4 Atwood offers a vision of the dual nature of people, houses, appearances and more: dark and light. Do you share her vision? If not, why not?

5 Looking back, can you identify clues throughout the novel that foreshadowed certain events? Share some examples from your own life where you might not have been surprised had you been able to spot some clues along the way.

6 How are the characters in this story — especially Simon Jordan — affected by the things they don't know?

7 Were you of the same mind regarding Grace's innocence or guilt throughout the novel? At what points did you waver one way or the other?

8 Did any character in the novel freely choose his or her course of action?

9 Why do you suppose the book is titled *Alias Grace?*

BECOMING NATIVE TO THIS PLACE

Author: Wes Jackson

Publisher: Counterpoint, 1996

Available in:
Quality paperback, 122 pages. $12.50
(ISBN 1-887178-11-2)

Genre: Nonfiction/Environment

Summary

In these essays, Jackson urges modern Americans to become "native to this place," to base our culture and agriculture on nature's principles, and to recycle as natural ecosystems have done for millions of years. Jackson suggests using dying small towns and rural communities as the foundation for a new kind of ecological economy. By operating on a set of assumptions and aspirations that are different from those of their ancestors, this new generation of pioneers can dig in and reclaim the land.

Recommended by: *Utne Reader*

"Jackson's ideas about growing roots and nourishing soul and soil are neither anachronistic nor romantic; they're based on hard-won practical experience — and, more often than not, are right on the mark."

Author Biography

Wes Jackson — a respected advocate for sustainable practices, organic agriculture, and environmental scientific understanding — is the founder of The Land Institute in Salina, Kansas. He and his research staff are at work on "the problem of agriculture," seeking to use native prairie as a model for a renewable farming economy. The author of ***Altars of Unhewn Stone*** and ***New Roots for Agriculture***, he was awarded a MacArthur Fellowship in 1992.

Topics to Consider

1   How does the author envision our connection to our natural and social environments?

2   What does "becoming native to this place" mean to you?

3   How can individuals and communities determine how best to balance the roles of technology and nature?

4   Discuss the theory of interpenetration that Jackson presents in Chapter Two.   How does an evolutionary/ecologically-based world view compare with a knowledge-based view?

5   Is it realistic to think that our society could ever embrace a standard of life that emphasizes neither efficiency nor production? If so, what would it take to get to that point?

6   What are the pitfalls of establishing a functional method that draws heavily on a prehistoric model?

7   As the author outlines it, what causes our dependence on an "extractive" economy?   What steps can we take to move away from this dependence?   How can we combat corporate-driven consumption?   Which of Jackson's ideas and theories do you feel is most applicable and/or relevant to our society?   To your particular community?

8   Give examples of a "science-state alignment."   How is this alignment positive?   Or negative?

9   Jackson suggests that we move from an economic organizing structure to an ecologically-based structure.   Do you think that the two are mutually exclusive?

10 Explain nature as a standard of measure.   What does this mean, and how does it relate to Jackson's experiment?

11 Can Jackson's experiment ever become more than just that?   If so, what would it take to bring it out of the fray to make it work?

BEYOND THE WHITENESS OF WHITENESS
Memoir of a White Mother of Black Sons

Author: Jane Lazarre

Publisher: Duke University Press, 1996

Available in:
Hardcover, 141 pages. $17.95
(ISBN 0-8223-1826-1)

Genre: Nonfiction/Autobiography

Summary

A moving account of life in a biracial family, this book is a powerful meditation on motherhood and racism in America, the story of an education into the realities of African-American culture. Recalling events that opened her eyes to her sons' and husband's experience as Black Americans — or her own revealing missteps — Lazarre describes a movement from silence to voice, to a commitment to action, and to an appreciation of the value of a fluid, even ambiguous identity. It is a coming of age that permits a final retelling of family history and family reunion, an incisive account of how perceptions of racial difference lie at the heart of the history and culture of America.

Recommended by: Sara Ruddick

" ... *Through maternal, autobiographical reflection, Jane Lazarre confronts the white racism that has shaped American society and remains our harshest tragedy and deepest challenge.*"

Author Biography

Jane Lazarre is Director of the Writing Program and Professor of Writing and Literature at Eugene Lang College, at the New School for Social Research. Her books include *The Mother Knot*, a memoir, the novels *Some Kind of Innocence, The Powers of Charlotte,* and *Worlds Beyond My Control,* and a volume of essays, *On Loving Men.*

Topics to Consider

1   What effects does the historical reality of slavery have on our lives today?

2   Lazarre describes herself as having been raised to be "color blind." As an adult, what does she discover about "color blindness" and its link to "the whiteness of whiteness?" What were you brought up to believe about racial differences?

3   Describe some of the hidden privileges of "whiteness."

4   What do you think of Lazarre's support for her sons' identities as Black men?

5   The book opens with Lazarre's visit to the Richmond Museum of the Confederacy. How did it affect you?

6   What does the author mean by "passing over?" What does she mean when she says, "I am no longer white. However I may appear to others, I am a person of color now."? Can you imagine circumstances besides marrying into a Black American family that would allow such a conversion to take place?

7   The author allows several different voices to speak in her book. What are the different voices? How does the author use them? Are some more successful than others?

8   What is your perspective on race in America? Did this book change that perspective at all? How so?

CHILDREN OF THE NIGHT
The Best Short Stories by Black Writers, 1967 to the Present

Editor: Gloria Naylor

Publisher: Back Bay Books, 1995
(Little, Brown and Company)

Available in:
Hardcover, 566 pages. $24.95
(ISBN 0-316-59926-3)
Quality paperback, 592 pages. $14.95
(ISBN 0-316-59923-9))

Genre: Fiction/Black Studies

Summary

In this landmark anthology — the companion volume to Langston Hughes's 1967 classic, *The Best Short Stories by Black Writers* — Gloria Naylor presents the finest African-American short stories of the last three decades. Arranged in four thematic sections — "Remembering," "Affirming," "Revealing the Self Divided," and "Moving On" — the thirty-seven stories included capture the many facets of the black experience in America. Featured are works by Maya Angelou, James Baldwin, Terry McMillan, and Ntozake Shange, among many others.

Recommended by: *Booklist*

"In this brilliant collection of superb writing, each story provides keen insights told in heartbreakingly beautiful prose."

Author Biography

Gloria Naylor won the National Book Award for *The Women of Brewster Place*. She is also the author of the novels *Mama Day, Bailey's Cafe,* and *Linden Hills,* as well as many short stories. She lives in Brooklyn, New York.

Topics to Consider

1   Does a reader read in 'color'? How significant is racial identity to the authors? To readers?

2   What section of the book did you relate to the most — *Remembering, Affirming, Revealing the Self Divided,* or *Moving On?* Why?

3   Which author's short story did you like the most? Why? Which one the least?

4   In *"The Tale of Gorgik,"* does Delany seem to suggest that there are degrees of slavery on every social level?

5   In Andrea Lee's *"Mother,"* what made the relationship between mother and daughter so unique?

6   In *"The Diary of an African Nun,"* do you think that the Sister is content with her lot in life? How is one able to experience contentment regardless of life's circumstances?

7   Ntozake Shange writes in dialect with no capitalization in *"oh she gotta head fulla hair."* How 'foreign' was the language to you? Is there any relationship between dialect and the recent 'ebonics' movement in California?

8   Did Edwidge Danticat's *"New York Day Women"* leave you wanting to know more about this mother and daughter and why they did what they did? How does their relationship compare to other mother-daughter relationships in the book? In your life?

A CIVIL ACTION

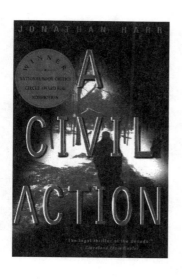

Author: Jonathan Harr

Publisher: Vintage Books, 1996

Available in:
Quality paperback, 512 pages. $13.00
(ISBN 0-679-77267-7)

Genre: Nonfiction/Current Affairs

Summary

In 1982, a young lawyer named Jan Schlichtmann took a case against his better judgment. Two of the nation's largest corporations stood accused of the deaths of children in a Massachusetts suburb; Schlichtmann hoped that a civil action might win his bereaved clients millions of dollars and make him rich and famous in the process. But over the next nine years, he found himself locked in an epic struggle that cost him his home, his reputation, and very nearly his sanity. The author was present at every stage of the proceedings; his legal reportage is at once the story of an emotionally explosive lawsuit and a searing exposé of the American legal system.

Recommended by: John Grisham

"Whether in truth or fiction, I have never read a more compelling chronicle of litigation."

Author Biography

Jonathan Harr lives and works in Northampton, MA, where he has taught nonfiction writing at Smith College. He is a former staff writer at *New England Monthly* and has written for *The New Yorker* and *The New York Times Magazine*. Harr spent nine years researching and writing *A Civil Action,* which was nominated for a National Book Award.

Topics to Consider

1 How important is personal honor to the characters, especially those in the face of possibly losing their jobs?

2 What do you think about Anne Anderson's decision not to go to Toronto with her husband? Would you have made the same decision?

3 Would any parent of a small child be able to decide the case on the evidence rather than emotion? Facher thinks that men would have less trouble than women. Do you agree?

4 How important is money in winning a suit?

5 Do you find Schlichtmann's dealings with the eight Woburn families to have been sufficiently fair and honest? Did he use them as a vehicle for his own ambition, fame and fortune?

6 Do you think the Woburn families were more interested in money, or in relieving their guilt?

7 The author suggests that perhaps the case was one "that the judicial system was not equipped to handle" (p. 369). Do you agree? How else could it have been handled — and settled?

8 Does courtroom rhetoric serve to reveal or to obscure the truth?

9 Could you have served as a juror in this case? Would your decision be the same? After their decision, the jurors each "had some misgivings, but on balance they felt they had done the best they could" (p. 392). Is that good enough?

10 Does the final settlement represent a victory, a loss, or a compromise?

11 What were your reactions toward Jan Schlichtmann as a lawyer? As a person?

12 Has reading this book changed your ideas about the American judiciary system, and, if so, in what way?

THE CLOISTER WALK

Author: Kathleen Norris

Publisher: Riverhead Books, 1996

Available in:
Hardcover, 384 pages. $23.95
(ISBN 1-57322-028-0)
Quality paperback, 400 pages. $12.00
(ISBN 1-57322-584-3)

Genre: Nonfiction/Spirituality

Summary

Why would a married woman with a thoroughly Protestant background and often more doubt than faith be drawn to the ancient practice of monasticism, to a community of celibate men whose days are centered around a rigid schedule of prayer, work, and scripture? This is the question that Norris herself asks as she found herself on two extended residencies at a Benedictine monastery. She shows us, from the rare perspective of someone who is both insider and outsider, how immersion in the cloistered world — its liturgy, its rituals, its sense of community — can impart meaning to everyday events and deepen our secular lives.

Recommended by: *The New York Times Book Review*

"Norris has a poet's particular eye, as well as a sense of humor and genuine social acuity."

Author Biography

Kathleen Norris is an award-winning poet and the author of *Dakota: A Spiritual Geography,* as well as three volumes of poetry. A recipient of grants from the Bush and Guggenheim foundations, she has been in residence twice at the Institute for Ecumenical and Cultural Research at St. John's Abbey in Collegeville, Minnesota, and has been, for ten years, an oblate of Assumption Abbey in North Dakota. She and her husband, the poet David Dwyer, live in South Dakota.

Topics to Consider

1 What do you think motivated Kathleen Norris to spend time at the monastery? What did she gain? Would you ever consider a similar course of action?

2 How did the retelling of her experience affect you, if at all? Were there any negative aspects to her experience?

3 How would you describe The Rule of St. Benedict? How does it balance the communal with the individual? What is the reason for the monks' communal lifestyle?

4 How is the Benedictine concept of time distinct? Are there any practical applications for secular life?

5 Norris includes a quotation from John Keats setting forth the concept of negative capability. Explain this idea and examine the value of such a tolerance of mystery. What do the Benedictines teach about this realm of thinking and feeling?

6 What special qualities does Norris find in the words of the Psalms and the Prophets? Compare and contrast the messages that Norris finds in these portions of the Bible.

7 The conventional definition of celibacy focuses on aspects of denial. After her experience with the monks, why does Norris see it instead as a source of freedom and of hospitality?

8 How would you characterize Norris's personal spirituality? What is distinctive about it? How would you describe your own?

9 What does this book have to say about the relationship between faith and doubt?

10 A number of books have appeared in recent years on the topic of simplifying one's life. What contribution does this book make to that movement? Are there ways that you feel similarly drawn to simplifying your life?

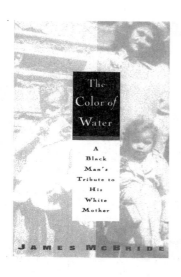

THE COLOR OF WATER
A Black Man's Tribute to His White Mother

Author: James McBride

Publisher: Riverhead Books, 1996

Available in:
Hardcover, 244 pages. $22.95
(ISBN 1-57322-022-1)
Quality paperback, 320 pages. $12.00
(ISBN 1-57322-578-9)

Genre: Nonfiction/Memoir

Summary

James McBride grew up one of twelve siblings in the all-black housing projects of Red Hook, Brooklyn, the son of a black minister and a woman who would not admit she was white. The object of McBride's constant embarrassment and continuous fear for her safety, his mother was an inspiring figure. McBride was an adult before he discovered the truth about his mother: The daughter of a failed itinerant Orthodox rabbi in rural Virginia, she had run away to Harlem, married a black man, and founded an all-black Baptist church in her living room. Around her narrative, McBride has written a portrait of growing up, a meditation on race and identity, and a poignant, beautifully crafted hymn from a son to his mother.

Recommended by: Jill Nelson

*"Full of laughter, insight, pain, understanding, and great love, **The Color of Water** transcends race and touches the spirit."*

Author Biography

James McBride, a writer and musician, is a former staff writer for *The Boston Globe, People* magazine, and *The Washington Post.* A professional saxophonist and composer, he has received the American Music Theater Festival's Stephen Sondheim Award for his work in musical theater composition. He lives in South Nyack, NY.

Topics to Consider

1 The author writes of being ashamed of his mother. Aren't all children ashamed of their parent(s) at times? How and why are the author's feelings out-of-the-ordinary?

2 What does the author's imaginary boy in the mirror really represent in childhood? In adulthood?

3 All Ruth's children seemed to run from their mother. Why? What was more of a factor, her race or her personality?

4 Ruth raised her children in black communities but sent them to predominantly white schools. Why? Do you agree with her actions?

5 Ruth's stern upbringing seems to have quite an impact on the way she disciplines her children. Should she have shared more of her background with her children? Would it have affected their respect for her and her rules?

6 How would you explain Ruth's zealousness for her new religion?

7 Ruth's father was a cruel, abusive human being. What influence does the relationship with a parent have on one's choosing a spouse?

8 How would you explain Ruth's attraction to black men?

9 Ruth's low self-esteem seems to have isolated her in adulthood. Why?

10 Ruth's family disowned her for being in love with a black man. Did it surprise you to find such intolerance between one minority group and another? What circumstances might push the limits of tolerance if it involved your own children?

11 The author seemed to become more tolerant of his mother after talking to people she knew when she was an adolescent. What did he learn that made a difference? What can *we* learn about becoming more tolerant of others?

12 How has our society's attitudes toward people of mixed heritage changed over generations?

CREEK WALK
and other stories

Author: Molly Giles

Publisher: Papier-Mache Press, 1997

Available in:
Hardcover, 144 pages. $23.00
(ISBN 1-57601-023-6)

Genre: Fiction

Summary

Molly Giles artfully weaves stories of women struggling to emerge into their truest natures as they reach out, change their lives, and save themselves. These women break the old patterns that have held them back and kept them silent. There are stories about love, relationships, violence, and careers, which stir an intense sense of recognition in women and their desire to communicate — to strangers much of their lives — and now to friends who are really listening and indelibly changed through this experience. Giles shares insights into the comic and tragic nature of life, the unflagging spirit to survive.

Recommended by: Amy Tan

"... Like the best fiction, these short stories seem deceptively smooth, at times, almost glib. But the core is pure Giles: disturbing, compassionate, and vital."

Author Biography

Molly Giles's first collection, ***Rough Translations,*** was nominated for the Pulitzer Prize and received the Flannery O'Conner Award for Fiction and *Boston Globe* Award, among others. Her fiction has been widely published in journals and magazines. Giles won the National Book Critics Circle Citation for Excellence in Book Reviewing in 1991. She is an associate professor of creative writing at San Francisco State University, and lives in Woodacre, California. As a writing professor, Giles has taught famous writers such as Amy Tan and Gus Lee.

Topics to Consider

1   In "The Writers' Model," what does the story say about how men and women communicate? Do you agree with the main character who feels she failed? Did she have to take off her clothes? How do the interview questions reflect the male perspective?

2   In "Survival in the Wilderness," why does Sherry search for evidence that can only destroy her relationship? Should she give Henry a second chance? How do you feel about "second chances" in general?

3   In "Leaving the Colonel," do you think the main character is crazy? Who is the "interviewer"? What role does the interviewer play?

4   Many of the women protagonists seem to have a hard time being heard. How much of their difficulties are their own fault? How much is related to society's expectations?

5   How would you characterize the romantic relationship in these stories? Which ones, if any, could you most identify with?

6   Why do you think Harriet in "Beginning Lessons" decided to talk to the woman on the bus? How do you think their conversation will change Harriet's life? Has your life been similarly impacted by a chance encounter?

7   In "Talking to Strangers," what effect does speaking in the first person have on the reader? How would the message of the story be different if told by her boyfriend?

8   In "Untitled," how does Ellen's search for direction affect her relationship with her writing students?

9   Do you think couples with different political and moral values can maintain a happy relationship?

10 Identify the ways several characters express control when their lives seem out of control. In what ways do you express control when your life seems chaotic? How are men and women different in this regard?

11 In "Talking to Strangers," a woman's career was secondary to her husband's career. Have you seen a change of attitude toward professional women in our society? Give some examples.

THE CRIMSON EDGE
Older Women Writing

Editor: Sondra Zeidenstein

Publisher: Chicory Blue Press, 1996

Available in:
Quality paperback, 282 pages. $16.95
(ISBN 1-887344-01-2)

Genre: Anthology/Creative Writing

Summary

The Crimson Edge is an anthology of fiction, memoir and poetry by seven women writers past the age of sixty. The subject matter includes: the relationship of a mother and her schizophrenic daughter; an African-American woman's experience of life in the North and South over a period of eighty years; flight from Nazi Germany to refugee life in the United States; life in a convent and the impetus to leave it after eighteen years; the split psyche of a closeted lesbian. Each author's creative writing is followed by an Afterword in which she talks about what is currently on her mind as an artist: what pressures to remain silent she's had to overcome, what remains to be done, etc.

Recommended by: Carolyn G. Heilbrun

"Not only are these seven women wonderful writers and poets, their accounts of coming to truth at this vital stage in life are mesmerizing ... a revolutionary book!"

Author Biography

Sondra Zeidenstein, who lives in Goshen, CT, is a poet, editor and publisher of Chicory Blue Press which is committed to supporting and encouraging risk-taking writing by older women writers. She is editor of *A Wider Giving: Women Writing after a Long Silence.* She has a Ph.D. in American literature from Columbia University and has taught in New York, Kathmandu and Dhaka.

Topics to Consider

1   What do these older women writers have to offer that would be hard for younger writers to imitate?

2   All the writers (whose average age is 73) write about mothers and children in some part of their work. Does it seem as if our feelings about mother/child relationships never go away?

3   Several of the authors address aspects of love and sex. Were you surprised to find sex so prevalent in older women's writing? Is what they have to say any different from younger writers?

4   In *A Stranger Here, Myself,* a white "liberal" narrator reveals her own racism. How does such a story complement the writing of Carrie Allen McCray, who has been the victim of such racism?

5   Anneliese Wagner writes about a period of her life that she cannot remember at all. She uses facts derived from photographs, visits, tales her mother tells her about their early years. Yet, there is no doubt she has captured the emotional truth of her escape from Germany and refugee experience. What does such a feat say about the imagination and its ability to "make up" the truth?

6   In her Afterword, Tema Nason talks about the obligation of her generation of mothers to tell their truths about motherhood, so that subsequent generations won't have to suffer the sense of failure and guilt that hers has. What do you think her story, *Full Moon,* contributes to that possibility?

7   In her Afterword, Sondra Zeidenstein writes about how hard it has been for her to fight the censoring voice in her that wants her to keep silent about certain subjects. Do you think there is anything an older woman writer should not write about? Or might have great difficulty in writing about? If you were a writer, of any age, what would you consider taboo, because of your own feelings or others?

8   Based on their creative work, and on what they have to say in the Afterwords, what do these writers have in common? What do you learn from them about the task of being a writer and the effect of age on their work?

9   Who are your favorite older women writers? Why?

"Delightful . . . both slam-bang and subtle."
— *The New York Times Book Review*

A novel by Lynne McFall

DANCER WITH BRUISED KNEES

Author: Lynne McFall

Publisher: Chronicle Books, 1994

Available in:
Quality paperback, 216 pages. $11.95
(ISBN 0-8118-1259-6)

Genre: Fiction

Summary

This is the hilarious tale of tough and witty Sarah Blight, a photographer braving her fortieth birthday which she says, launched her into "a depression so deep that not even the thought of sex could raise me from it." Her heartrending and hilarious account of life, past and present, makes *Dancer with Bruised Knees* an unpredictable, outrageous, and very seductive novel.

Recommended by: Robert Boswell

"Without apology, without sentimentality, this dark and viciously funny novel chronicles the worst year in a rough life, forcing the reader to laugh at each disaster. With taut, eloquent language and heart-stopping honesty, Lynne McFall creates a vision of the world that will make readers squirm and clutch at their chairs. "

Author Biography

Lynne McFall teaches philosophy at Syracuse University and lives the rest of the year in Montana. Her fiction has appeared in the *New England Review/Bread Loaf Quarterly, Prairie Schooner, Between C&D,* and *Other Voices.* Her first novel, *The One True Story of the World,* was published to wide praise in 1990.

Topics to Consider

1   Did you have a brother that tormented you? How is Sarah's brother like him and not like him?

2   Do you see Sarah as a product of her family background? How do Sarah's parents' addictions and phobias define how the family functions?

3   How does the concept of bipolar disorder affect the pacing of the book, if at all? Does Sarah's being on Prozac change her voice?

4   Does Sarah's violent streak at the end of the book come as a surprise? Is she responsible for her actions?

5   A lot of terrible things happen in this book, yet it's funny. Why? In what ways do tragedy and humor go hand-in-hand?

6   Compare and contrast the sisters' outlook on life.

7   What do you think of the men in Sarah's life, especially Sunny and Jake?

8   What does McFall want us to understand about vision, photographs, and memory?

THE ENGLISH PATIENT

Author: Michael Ondaatje

Publisher: Vintage International, 1993

Available in:
Quality paperback, 320 pages. $12.00
(ISBN 0-679-74520-3)

Genre: Fiction/Literature

Summary

It is 1944, and the war in central Italy is over, leaving in its wake a landscape of ruined places and people. In an isolated villa, two people remain: a young Canadian nurse, Hana, almost destroyed by war and the death of her father, and her last patient, a man burned beyond recognition, who drifts in and out of his own memories and dreams. Into their lives comes Caravaggio, a thief who has been tortured and maimed by wartime inquisitors, and Kip, a young Sikh who has spent the war dismantling bombs. The four protagonists carry on a remote, intensely personal existence, as they play out their interior drama.

Recommended by: *Time Magazine*

" ... a rare and spellbinding web of dreams."

Author Biography

Michael Ondaatje was born in Ceylon (now Sri Lanka), was educated in London and Quebec, and received his BA from the University of Toronto in 1965. Since 1971, he has been a member of the English Department at Glendon College in Toronto. A prolific author not only of fiction but of poetry and nonfiction, Ondaatje's other books include *The Collected Works of Billy the Kid, Coming Through Slaughter,* and *Running in the Family.* He has been awarded many prizes, including the Booker Prize, England's highest honor for fiction.

Topics to Consider

1   Why does the patient consider himself to have "died" (p. 4)? Does he undergo any kind of rebirth during the course of the story?

2   How can feelings about a parent, such as Hana's for her father, affect relationships with significant others?

3   Why did Hana decide to have an abortion during the war? How did that decision affect her?

4   Caravaggio has avoided permanent intimacy all his life (p. 116). Does he ever come to accept intimacy, and if so, in what form and with whom?

5   How does the subject of race and racism enter into this novel? What conclusions, if any, are drawn at the end?

6   Why do you think that Hana removes all the mirrors in the house and puts them in an empty room?

7   How would you describe the connection between the English patient and Kip? Is it emotional, political, or dependent upon some other tie? What is the primary tie that connects you to others?

8   Out of similar disillusionment, Madox commits suicide while Kip is able to create a new life. What accounts for the difference?

9   When physical violence is present in a relationship, as it is between Katherine and her lover, what does that say about the relationship? Do you see any connection between sex and death, as Almasy seemed to do?

10 How do the characters discover or come to terms with their own identities?

THE *GAZETTE* GIRLS OF GRUNDY COUNTY
Horse Trading, Hot Lead, and High Heels

Authors:
Gwen Hamilton Thogmartin
Ardis Hamilton Anderson

Publisher: University of Missouri Press, 1994

Available in:
Hardcover, 184 pages. $19.95
(ISBN 0-8262-0986-6)

Genre: Biography/Americana

Summary

It was 1935 when Gwen and Ardis Hamilton, both barely old enough to vote, bought the *Grundy County Gazette*. Although both women had been trained in journalism, their education hadn't prepared them for the realities of running a country newspaper. Filled with hilarious stories of small-town life — in chapters that alternate between the sisters' distinctive voices — *The Gazette Girls* tells a captivating story of two women coming of age in the newspaper business and an extraordinary slice of Americana.

Recommended by: *Los Angeles Times Book Review*

" ... a thoroughly charming little memoir ... plus a pre-Lib primer on what a woman could do when she set her mind to it ... "

Authors' Biographies

After selling the *Grundy County Gazette* in 1938, **Gwen Hamilton Thogmartin** worked for Emporia State University and the Lyon County Historical Society Museum. Financial difficulties had made it impossible for her to complete her undergraduate studies in the early 1930s, but she completed her degree in 1975. **Ardis Hamilton Anderson** continued her work in journalism as a reporter. She was the youngest charter member of the Missouri Women's Press Club, in which she remained active until leaving the state in 1990. Both women now live in Emporia, Kansas, not far from their hometown of Waverly.

Topics to Consider

1 How do the approaches of the two sisters differ in their telling of the same story?

2 How have women's choices changed in the past sixty years? What obstacles did Gwen and Ardis have to overcome that women don't have to face today? In what ways were their lives easier?

3 Gwen says, "The soap operas have always been tame in comparison with the stories from life we unearthed, accidentally and in the line of duty, while we were on the *Gazette.*" Which of the media do you find most credible when it comes to reporting the news?

4 How has the practice of journalism changed in the past sixty years? Does the type of one-on-one journalism that Ardis and Gwen practiced still exist today? To what extent do you think that television and other forms of entertainment and technology have replaced one-on-one contact in our society?

5 To what extent is it the role of a journalist to become familiar with and report on the private lives of people in the community?

6 Of the examples of ads and news stories reproduced from the *Gazette,* which is your favorite? Why?

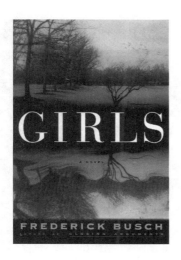

GIRLS

Author: Frederick Busch

Publisher: Harmony Books, 1997

Available in:
Hardcover, 288 pages. $23.00
(ISBN 0-517-70455-2)

Genre: Fiction

Summary

In the unrelentingly cold and bitter winter of upstate New York, Jack and his wife, Fanny, are trying to come to terms with the death of their young daughter. A chasm has formed in their relationship and Jack is looking for a way to heal them both.

Meanwhile, near the town where they live, a 14-year-old girl has disappeared between her parents' home and her father's church. Finding what has become of *this* child could be Jack's salvation, if he can just get to her in time.

Recommended by: *Seattle Times*

" ... *the classic American style, ice-clear, dagger-sharp, with dialogue that slashes back and forth like a razor.* "

Author Biography

Frederick Busch's most recent book was a finalist for the 1995 PEN/Faulkner Award. He is the author of *Closing Arguments* and a professor at Colgate University.

Topics to Consider

1 What does "seeing the flash" mean? Who sees it? Does "the flash" illuminate or disguise events?

2 Discuss the significance of Ralph the duck.

3 How does Jack's obsession with finding other lost girls help him deal with his own lost child? What is the connection between what happened to these girls and what happened to his own daughter?

4 How did baby Hannah die? Why does Jack shield his wife from her role in their daughter's death? What, if any, are the merits of his decision to withhold information? How would you expect the loss of a child to impact a relationship?

5 How does Jack's experience in the Vietnam war impact the choices he makes in his current life?

6 On pages 75-76, there is a discussion of serial killers and their motivation. How does a fear of "deadness" provoke death?

7 Discuss the juxtaposition of Fanny/Jack/Hannah with the secret service/library situation (see page 115). What are the similarities between Jack and the librarian? How are they both in a position to withhold and disclose information? Explain the respective choices they make.

8 What is the purpose of setting the multitude of tragedies which occur in *Girls* against the backdrop of a privileged college "playground?"

GOODNESS

Author: Martha Roth

Publisher: Spinsters Ink, 1996

Available in:
Quality paperback, 320 pages. $10.95
(ISBN 1-883523-11-7)

Genre: Fiction/Women's Studies

Summary

Goodness brings us into the lives of a close-knit group of midwestern feminists and peace activists, whose coming of age during the tumult of the '60s profoundly shapes the rest of their lives. The evolving relationships between friends and lovers, women and women, women and men, and mothers and their children are woven into a story of pain and discovery, of raising families and holding demonstrations, of fighting to change the world during an era of social upheaval, and of trying to maintain the idealism of the 1960s without succumbing to the cynicism of later years.

Recommended by: Tillie Olsen

"Indeed, the loving, caring, acting beings — so real, so unforgettable— who comprise this book shine like a beacon: reaffirming, inspiring, and steadying. I want everyone I love to read this book."

Author Biography

Martha Roth is founding editor of *Hurricane Alice: A Feminist Quarterly*. She is co-editor of the award-winning **Mother Journeys: Feminists Write About Mothering** (Spinsters Ink, 1994) and co-editor of **Transforming a Rape Culture** (Milkweed Editions, 1993). Ms. Roth lives in Minneapolis.

Topics to Consider

1   Why do you think **Goodness** is written in journal or memoir format? If only one character were to narrate the story of these friends and lovers, who would it be?

2   Why does Cora want to adopt a baby at this point in her life? Why does Dinah go to such lengths to try to obtain a baby for Cora?

3   The preparation of foods and grains is a central motif of **Goodness.** Discuss the scenes in which foods and grains play a role. What do foods and grains represent in these scenes and in the novel as a whole?

4   How would you describe Cora's relationship with her children? How does it compare to Dinah's relationship with her children?

5   What impact do Cora's and Dinah's political activities have on their children?

6   Do you like Dinah? Why or why not? What do you think Dinah wants from life?

7   What kinds of relationships do the women in the consciousness-raising group have with one another? Why?

8   What impact do the events of the '60s have on the main characters in their later lives?

9   What effect do the political activities of Cora, Dinah, and the others have on their world?

10 How does the world view of each main character (including Cora herself) color her or his reaction to Cora's terminal illness?

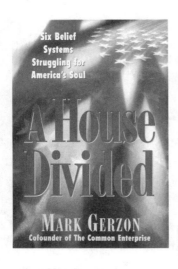

A HOUSE DIVIDED
Six Belief Systems Struggling for America's Soul

Author: Mark Gerzon

Publisher: Jeremy P. Tarcher/ Putnam, 1996

Available in:
Hardcover, 352 pages. $24.95
(ISBN 0-87477-823-9)
Quality paperback, 352 pages. $15.95
(ISBN 0-87477-874-3)

Genre: Current Events/Politics

Summary

On the eve of the Civil War, Abraham Lincoln warned: "A house divided against itself cannot stand." Today, more than a century later, *A House Divided* alerts us to the dangerous, increasingly vicious civil wars within our nation today, and offers firsthand accounts of those who are working to heal the wounds.

Unlike traditional commentaries on the "culture wars" that offer a one-dimensional liberal/conservative perspective, *A House Divided* fairly presents several opposing points of view and offers practical examples for those seeking to reclaim civility and decency in public discourse.

Recommended by: M. Scott Peck

"A brilliant, highly readable, desperately needed work that finally clarifies the meaning of citizenship and community. Hurrah!"

Author Biography

Mark Gerzon, a consultant to the Rockefeller Foundation, has worked for twenty years with a wide variety of organizations working to resolve community conflicts and revitalize citizenship. He is the author of several books, including *The Whole World is Watching, A Choice of Heroes,* and *Listening to Midlife.* He lives in Colorado with his wife and their three sons.

Topics to Consider

1   What does Gerzon mean by the Divided States of America?

2   The author identified six States or belief systems. Can you think of any others that might have been included?

3   Gerzon considers the media a belief system. Do you agree? Why or why not?

4   Can one live in different States at the same time?

5   In which State do you live?

6   Have the divisions in America gone too far? Can we really heal our deep wounds and reunite?

7   What can we do as citizens to help reunite America?

8   In the second half of the book, the author proposes a new patriotism. How is this different than traditional concepts of patriotism?

9   Can you give some examples of new patriots?

10 No matter how badly we may want to ease tensions among our fellow citizens, there are some issues on which there seems to be no room for compromise. How can we reconcile our desire to get along with our need to maintain our principles?

11 As we head into the next millennium, how can we best offer younger generations a sense of hope about America's future?

IN A FAMILY WAY

Author:
Rochelle Hollander Schwab

Publisher: Orlando Place Press, 1995

Available in:
Quality paperback, 316 pages, $10.95
(ISBN 0-9643650-0-6)

Genre: Fiction

Summary

Keith was disowned by his family when he came out as a gay man. Sonya lost custody of her children when her ex-husband discovered she was a lesbian. Now she and Janice have started a new family — with Keith's help as sperm donor. But when Janice, the birth mother, is tragically killed, baby Heather's future is left up to a family court — the result of a three-way struggle for custody between Sonya, Keith and grandparents bent on rescuing their grandchild from a "homosexual lifestyle." This book was termed "a thought-provoking novel that probes the complexity of the word 'family'" by *Small Press.*

Recommended by: *San Francisco Chronicle*

" ... a vivid evocation of family life, and a real page-turner."

Author Biography

Rochelle Schwab lives with her husband in Alexandria, Virginia, and is the author of two previous novels, ***As Far as Blood Goes*** and ***A Different Sin***. The mother of two grown daughters, and a proud grandmother, she's active in PFLAG (Parents, Families and Friends of Lesbians and Gays). Her work in PFLAG and her relationship with her lesbian daughter and her friends have broadened her concept of "family" and spurred her to a fictional exploration of nontraditional family issues.

Topics to Consider

1 Why did Keith's partner, Aaron, argue against donating sperm to Janice and Sonya? Why did Keith decide to do so? Which one was right, and why?

2 Keith signed an agreement waiving all parental rights to any resultant child in advance of donating sperm. Did he give sufficient thought to the possibility that he would have a change of heart once the baby was born? Did Janice or Sonya? Was it fair of them to exclude the baby's biological father from her life?

3 What would be your community's reaction to a custody case involving gay or lesbian parents? What are your own feelings about the rights of lesbians and gays to form families?

4 Courts in several states have allowed a spouse of the same sex to adopt his/her partner's child, without forcing the biological parent to waive his or her own rights. Would this have been a good route for Sonya? What are your feelings about the legalization of same-sex marriages?

5 Aaron's desire to see Sonya's parental rights accorded legal status leads him to support Sonya and even testify against Keith at the custody hearing. Not surprisingly, this hurts Keith and makes any reconciliation between the two men less likely. How would you have handled this situation if you were Aaron?

6 Under what circumstances do couples, whether gay or straight, tolerate strains in their relationship? What precipitates a final breakup?

7 Keith tries to assure Janice's mother that he will see to it "that Heather has a perfectly normal childhood." What is a normal childhood?

8 Sonya's attorney asks the judge to set new legal precedent by accepting Sonya and Janice's relationship as making them — in Janice's words — "a real family." What do you consider a "real family?" What relationships do you have that you consider "family?"

9 Do you have gay or lesbian members in your family? How would you describe your family's reaction? How might you react if one of your children, or a close family member, "came out" to you as lesbian or gay?

INDEPENDENCE DAY

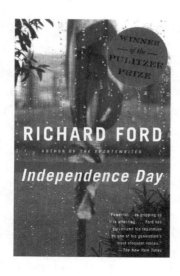

Author: Richard Ford

Publisher: Vintage Books, 1996

Available in:
Quality paperback, 464 pages. $13.00
(ISBN 0-679-73518-6)

Genre: Fiction/Literature

Summary

In this sequel to *The Sportswriter,* Frank Bascombe — now forty-four, divorced, "residential specialist," former sportswriter, parent, Democrat, and occasional Presbyterian with a fear of "disappearing" — finds his life at a "turning or at least a curving point" on the Fourth of July weekend, 1988. He collects his troubled teenage son, Paul, for a weekend trip to several sports halls of fame. Their journey — a passage through choices, reflections, and regrets — is transformed in one lightning-bolt moment alongside a peaceful baseball field. Helped by a solicitous stranger, Frank and his son are carried across their own spiritual deep river to a fresh start on the other side.

Recommended by: *Washington Times*

" ... A bold, clear-eyed, ambitious, original and wickedly funny take on American life ..."

Author Biography

Richard Ford briefly attended law school before he received his M.F.A. in writing in 1970. His novel, *The Sportswriter,* was named one of five best books of 1986 by *Time* magazine. Other books include *A Piece of My Heart* (1976), *The Ultimate Good Luck* (1981), *Rock Springs* (1987), and *Wildlife* (1990). *Independence Day* won the Pulitzer Prize and the PEN/Faulkner Award for fiction, the first novel ever to win both awards. Ford lives in New Orleans with his wife of twenty-eight years, Kristina. He also spends time on a plantation and at his cabin in Montana.

Topics to Consider

1 Haddam, New Jersey, is introduced as idyllic, but reality soon counters the idyll. How does Independence Day's catalog of past and present Americana juxtapose the ideal and the real? Does the novel express the American character?

2 His ex-wife, Ann, calls him cynical. His girlfriend, Sally, finds him "too smooth" and "non-committal." Frank says, "I'm no hero." What kind of person *is* he? In what ways *is* he heroic?

3 How is Clarissa affected by the divorce? How does the novel mourn the loss of the nuclear family?

4 Are the Markhams "out-of-the-ordinary white folks" in their racial outlook? How representative of Americans are they?

5 How does Frank come to define "progress?" Would your definition be any different? Do the weekend's events chronicle Frank's spiritual growth as a kind of "progress?"

6 Irv appears out of the blue when Paul is struck. Who *is* Irv? How does he minister to Frank? How do people like Irv fare in today's world?

7 How is Paul's accident a catalyst for change? How does Paul's eye injury alter Frank's vision?

8 When is the reconciliation of past and present warranted? In Frank's case, was reconciliation ever accomplished?

9 "I *don't* believe in God," Frank insists. Karl answers, "You *seem* one way and *are* another." How would you have answered? What stands in the way of Frank's belief in God?

10 Real estate is a central metaphor in the book. Who are the metaphorical tenants and landlord? Is any form of shelter *not* described? How would you respond to Frank's comment, "What more can you do for wayward strangers than to shelter them?"

11 What does "Independence Day" really mean for Frank? Have you ever experienced a similar feeling?

INFINITE JEST

Author: David Foster Wallace

Publisher: Back Bay Books, 1996
(Little, Brown and Company)

Available in:
Hardcover, 1,079 pages. $29.95
(ISBN 0-316-92004-5)
Quality paperback, 1,088 pages. $14.95
(ISBN 0-316-92117-3)

Genre: Fiction

Summary

Set in a drug and alcohol addicts' halfway house and a tennis academy, and featuring the most endearingly screwed-up family to come our way since the Glasses, *Infinite Jest* is a gargantuan, mind-altering comedy about the Pursuit of Happiness in America. It explores essential questions about what entertainment is and why it has come to so dominate our lives; about how our desire for entertainment interacts with our need to connect with other humans; and about what the pleasures we choose say about who we are.

Equal parts philosophical quest and screwball comedy, *Infinite Jest* bends every rule of fiction without sacrificing for a moment its own entertainment value. It is an exuberant, uniquely American exploration of the passions that make us human — and one of those rare books that renews the idea of what a novel can do.

Recommended by: Sven Birkerts, *Atlantic Monthly*

"... Edgy, accurate, and darkly witty ... Think Beckett, think Pynchon, think Gaddis. Think."

Author Biography

David Foster Wallace is the award-winning author of *The Broom of the System* and *Girl with Curious Hair*. His stories have appeared in the *New Yorker, Harper's,* and the *Paris Review.* He teaches English at Illinois State University and lives in Bloomington, Illinois.

Topics to Consider

1   Wallace outlines a variety of addictions — from substance abuse to obsessive behavior. How are these addictions similar in form and how are they different? Does your definition of what comprises an addiction change after reading this book?

2   The two primary institutions of focus in Wallace's novel are Ennett House (a rehabilitation facility) and the Enfield Tennis Academy. What do their respective inhabitants have in common? How are the individuals in each facility at once slaves to themselves and part of something larger?

3   Both Ennett House and the Enfield Tennis Academy, though different in purpose, are highly structured institutions with set rules and requirements. How does this structure affect the individuals involved? Do you think that a great deal of structure facilitates movement towards a specific goal, or does it cause stagnation?

4   Where does the will of the individual end and the will of the institution take over? Are the characters able to maintain this distinction for themselves?

5   How do life's addictions, whether they be to material goods, certain behaviors or substances, create cages? How does one escape from the cage? Discuss the cages as they exist for the major characters in *Infinite Jest.*

6   Discuss the concept of entertainment. What makes something entertaining? What role does "The Entertainment" play in *Infinite Jest?* Wallace draws a fine line between entertainment and obsession. Do you agree with this characterization? Can something which is entertaining, by definition, be psychically numbing?

MAMA'S GIRL

Author: Veronica Chambers

Publisher: Riverhead Books, 1996

Available in:
Hardcover, 194 pages. $22.95
(ISBN 1-57322-030-2)
Quality paperback, 208 pages. $12.00
(ISBN 1-57322-599-1)

Genre: Nonfiction/Memoir

Summary

More than a family memoir, *Mama's Girl* gives voice to the first generation of African-Americans to come of age in the post-Civil Rights era. Chambers's account of her relationship with her mother brings to life all the promise, conflict, and unanswered questions that accompany this time: how to navigate the gulf between a mother's hopes and a daughter's ambition; how to leave home without leaving behind those you love; how to accept what you've been given when you want more than your mother can give. *Mama's Girl* tells the story of a daughter's resolute journey toward self-discovery, under-standing, forgiveness, and, for her mother, a love supreme.

Recommended by: Bebe Moore Campbell

" ... for any daughter who has ever loved and blamed Mama in the same anguished breath, ever pushed Mama away while yearning for her embrace."

Author Biography

Veronica Chambers is a former editor at *The New York Times Magazine* and *Premiere,* and is currently a contributing editor at *Glamour,* where she was named one of the top ten college women of 1990. She is the co-author, with John Singleton, of *Poetic Justice,* and a frequent contributor to a number of publications. Chambers, who has held a Freedom Forum Fellowship at Columbia University, lives in Brooklyn, New York.

Topics to Consider

1 In what sense is Veronica Chambers a "mama's girl"? Can the same be said of all women?

2 In the acknowledgment, Chambers thanks her mother for "not minding that I put all of our business on the street." If you were her mother, how would you feel about the book?

3 In chapter one, Chambers, as a child trying to get her mother's attention, thinks "it's always some other time with her." Yet she reveals that to her "my mother is everything." How can these feelings co-exist?

4 What lessons did Chambers learn from the men in her life? What hold did they have on her, especially her father?

5 Chambers believed that "one day, I was going to make it out of these bad neighborhoods and these piss-poor schools where I had to beg for real work. I knew my mother wasn't going to help me, even if I didn't know why." Where did Veronica's determination come from? Why didn't her mother support her?

6 On what does Chambers model her own behavior? Dreams, trust and charm all play a part in her environment growing up. What role do these factors play in her mature life?

7 Chambers concludes that "I am the woman I am today because of her" [her mother]. Given what the book reveals, how much truth do you see in this statement?

8 When Veronica's mother finally hugged her "and did not let go," did she redeem herself for the times she did not hug her or ask her to come home? Would redemption be at all available to her father?

9 What gifts does Veronica's mother give her? What does she with-hold? What did Veronica teach her mother?

10 What commentary does the story of Veronica Chambers make on the larger issue of nature versus nurture?

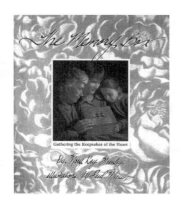

THE MEMORY BOX
Gathering the Keepsakes of the Heart

Author: Mary Kay Shanley

Publisher: Sta-Kris, 1996

Available in:
Hardcover (illustrated), 46 pages. $14.95
(ISBN 1-882835-32-8)

Genre: Inspiration/Gift

Summary

The box, fashioned from wood salvaged from the house where her father grew up, held treasures. A lion penny bank, an old wooden spoon, a dog collar. Memories that define who you are. *The Memory Box* combines a tender story by Mary Kay Shanley with rich illustrations by award-winning illustrator Paul Micich that portray one of life's most poignant transitions — the moment of saying good-bye to the past and the resulting sense of loss. However, the characters soon realize that memories never reside in places you live, not in things you've done, not in keepsakes you own. Rather, memories are in the heart of the keeper, and as such, truly become treasures to pass on to generations that follow.

Recommended by: Patty Beutler, *Lincoln Journal Star*

" ... *reminds us that memories are more than moments frozen in time — they represent values passed from one generation to another. This tender story will send you rummaging through your attic and your past.*"

Author Biography

Mary Kay Shanley has been a newspaper reporter, free-lance writer, and now, author. Her other books include *She Taught Me To Eat Artichokes* and *Little Lessons for Teachers.* She has edited a collection of essays from across America, *When I Think About My Father.* She lives in West Des Moines, Iowa.

Topics to Consider

1   The author believes that our memories are the key to who we are and what we are, even *why* we are. Do you agree? Why or why not?

2   One message in the book is that memories are treasured heirlooms that can — and should — be handed down from generation to generation. Is that something you do? If so, how?

3   Many of our memories are based on traditions we share with family and friends. Have you ever tried changing one of those traditions? What happened?

4   What is the value of encouraging our memories?

5   We all want to pass along what we value most to our children and other family members. What about our wider circle of friends and acquaintances? Is it important to share memories with them, too? Why?

6   Some of the memories the author cherished stemmed from moments in her past which — at the time — seemed insignificant. What memories do you treasure that arose from everyday life?

7   How can we treasure past events and people without preventing present-day growth and clutter?

8   How does the sharing of memories connect past with future?

9   Can memories, maxims, and meritorious behavior from generations past have relevance and value today?

10 How can you treasure a memory without treasuring the object?

11 What is the significance of the peony plant in the book? Are there "peony plants" in your life?

12 The daughter in the book understood that her mother and grandmother were passing on something of value to her. Do you recall how or when you first became aware that preceding generations were giving you values — and probably doing so with a dose of wisdom?

MIDWIVES

Author: Chris Bohjalian

Publisher: Harmony Books, 1997

Available in:
Hardcover, 320 pages. $24.00
(ISBN 0-517-70396-3)

Genre: Fiction

Summary

Reddington, Vermont, Winter 1981. Sybil Danforth, a talented midwife who specializes in home birth, is arrested for murder when she saves a baby during a brutal ice storm by performing a Caesarean section once she believes the mother has died, only to have her assistant insist afterward that the mother was still very much alive.

Narrated by Sibyl's daughter, Connie, now a respected obstetrician, *Midwives* depicts the aftermath of the tragedy. As the Danforth family, the town, and the reader are drawn into a gripping trial that at first appears meritless, and later frighteningly simple for Sibyl to lose, it is Connie's mesmerizing voice that keeps the pages turning.

Recommended by: Julia Alvarez

" ... a heck of a good read with a gripping plot ... elegantly structured and captivating."

Author Biography

Chris Bohjalian is the author of four acclaimed novels, including *Water Witches*. A weekly features columnist for the *Burlington Free Press* and a features writer for *The Boston Globe Sunday Magazine,* he lives in Lincoln, Vermont.

Topics to Consider

1   Sibyl's journal entries guide the course of the novel. Discuss how they become of monumental importance to both mother and daughter. How does Sibyl's private diary change her relationship with her daughter? Does its existence change the course of Connie's life? How has your own life been impacted, if at all, by the presence of a diary?

2   Connie becomes a licensed physician, indeed, an Ob-Gyn. Does her decision vindicate or reject her mother's choices? Is the novel in general a celebration or denunciation of home birth?

3   Does Sibyl make use of Stephen's attraction to her? How?

4   Discuss various birth options available to women, and the pros and cons of each.

5   Why do you think Asa and Charlotte chose home birth as an option when the birth of her first child had been complicated by hypertension?

6   How would you react if you were asked to be a juror at the trial? What kinds of people would have constituted an ideal jury for the defense?

7   Sibyl mentions her personal diaries at the trial. Was it a slip of the tongue? Or was it a more conscious attempt to sabotage the outcome? How did you feel about the verdict?

8   Sibyl seems to lose the joy of the midwifery experience. Why? Does she feel guilty? Unsure? Or something else entirely?

9   After you've finished the book, reread the quotes at the beginning. How has the meaning changed?

NO MATTER WHAT

Mary Saracino

Author: Mary Saracino

Publisher: Spinsters Ink, 1993

Available in:
Quality paperback, 320 pages. $9.95
(ISBN 0-933216-91-2)

Genre: Fiction/Coming of Age

Summary

This haunting story of family love and betrayal is narrated by 10-year-old Peanut. As the oldest daughter in her working-class Catholic family during the '60s, Peanut is proud to be her mother's confidante and right hand, but it is a heavy burden to bear. Peanut's mother, embroiled in an affair with a priest, is considering running away with him. Because of Peanut's parents' inability to deal honestly with the deterioration of their marriage, they fail to see the havoc their behavior is causing their five children.

Recommended by: Dorothy Allison

*"Unflinching, insightful, beautifully written, Mary Saracino's **No Matter What** is a terrible fable told from the child's perspective."*

Author Biography

Mary Saracino is a freelance writer and Shiatsu bodywork practitioner. Her work has appeared in several national and regional publications. Ms. Saracino lives in Minneapolis, where she is working on another novel about Peanut and her family.

Topics to Consider

1   What is the relationship between Marie and Peanut? Between Marie and her other daughters? Between Marie and her sons?

2   Describe Peanut's relationship with her father. How does it help or hinder her at crucial points in her life?

3   Examine the different ways in which the children respond to Patrick. What prompts their reactions, both initial and long-term?

4   How do you feel about Patrick and Marie's relationship? Paulie and Marie's? Do you think that if Marie leaves Paulie for Patrick, she will find happiness?

5   Examine key scenes in which the weather mirrors or affects the characters or scenes. What role does the weather play in each of these scenes?

6   The different members of the family each manage to bond to something or someone. Who or what does each person choose? What happens when these bonds are severed?

7   Catholicism is interpreted in different ways by the different characters. What seems to be Patrick and Marie's attitudes towards Catholicism and the Catholic Church? How do the children interpret Catholicism? How do the priests and nuns perceive themselves?

8   This book is part of a series "dedicated to focusing on pivotal moments or times in girls' or young women's lives." At this time in Peanut's life, what do you foresee for her future? Which factors are positive, and which ones negative? What avenues or choices are available to her that might effect a different outcome?

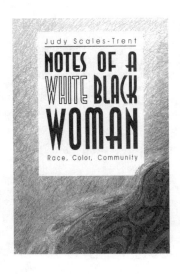

Judy Scales-Trent

NOTES OF A
WHITE BLACK
WOMAN
Race, Color, Community

NOTES OF A WHITE BLACK WOMAN
Race, Color, Community

Author: Judy Scales-Trent

Publisher: The Pennsylvania State University Press, 1995

Available in:
Hardcover, 200 pages. $19.50
(ISBN 0-271-01430-X)

Genre: Nonfiction/Autobiography

Summary

Notes of a White Black Woman describes a hidden part of the black experience in America by exploring what it is like to be a "white" black woman and to live simultaneously inside and outside of both white and black communities. By tracing how America's racial purity laws have operated over the past 400 years (creating a large group of black Americans with white skin), Scales-Trent explores the question of what we really mean by "race" in this country.

Recommended by: Martha Minow

" ... At turns gentle and angry, awed and critical, this is must reading for anyone interested in identity, race relations, civil rights, and the avenues for personal fulfillment."

Author Biography

Judy Scales-Trent teaches at the SUNY-Buffalo School of Law. Her father was the first Executive Director of the United Negro College Fund, and her grandfather was president of Livingstone College in Salisbury, NC, for 30 years. After receiving her law degree, she was a civil rights lawyer for ten years in Washington, DC. She has published widely in both legal journals and anthologies of black women writers.

Topics to Consider

1   The author defines a "white black person" as a black American with white skin, a person with both African and European ancestry. How does this definition differ from what you might have thought the term to mean before reading this book?

2   Black Americans with darker skin stereotyped the author because of her skin color. What other stereotypes can be invoked solely on the basis of appearance?

3   Because the issues of skin color and "passing" were never out in the open within the black community, the author found it easier to write about them than to talk about it. What other issues might feel more safe to write about first?

4   Have you known someone — or ever tried yourself — to pass as someone other than who they really were?

5   How has the "one-drop" rule — that if you have any ancestors at all from Africa, you are black — shaped our definition of race?

6   The author writes that one can be white and black at the same time. Do you agree? Why would this be helpful to the dialogue on race in America?

7   "Lost Great-Uncle Charles" was given a choice: (1) "If you live as a black person, then you can't do this work, you will be treated badly, you will fear for your life; or (2) "Live as a white person, and your life will be much better. Of course, you will have to leave all your loved ones in order to do this." What would you do, given such a cruel and difficult choice?

8   Can you relate to feeling forced to straddle two worlds?

9   Discuss "survival guilt," and how it can affect one's life.

10 How did this book affect your perception and judgment of others?

ONLY TWICE I'VE WISHED FOR HEAVEN

Author: Dawn Turner Trice

Publisher: Crown, 1997

Available in:
Hardcover, 336 pages. $23.00
(ISBN 0-517-70428-5)

Genre: Fiction

Summary

In 1975 young Tempestt Saville and her family are chosen by lottery to "move on up" to Lakeland: one square mile of rich black soil carved out of a Chicago ghetto, cradling sparkling apartment towers and emerald lawns where the elite of black professionals live in privilege, secure behind a 10-foot-tall ivy-covered fence.

But 11-year-old Tempestt is drawn to the world outside the fence, to 35th Street, a place of colorful, often dangerous, characters. Here the saved and the sinners are both so "done-up" you can't tell one from the other. Before a month has passed at Lakeland, Tempestt will witness the death of a friend, cause the arrest of a preacher, and start a chain of events that will send 35th Street up in flames.

Recommended by: Maya Angelou

"Only Twice I've Wished for Heaven is about fascinating people during turbulent times. Dawn Turner Trice has written a complicated story beautifully."

Author Biography

Dawn Turner Trice is an editor at the *Chicago Tribune* and was a participant of the Iowa Writers' Workshop. She lives in Moline, Illinois.

Topics to Consider

1   Discuss the title. Who, specifically, does the title refer to? What do the novel's major characters wish for? How do their definitions of heaven vary?

2   Birds and the role of flight serve as reoccurring themes both literally and metaphorically. Discuss the significance of the birds as they appear throughout the novel and explain the connection between flight and freedom. How is freedom different for each character?

3   Life seems to be more truly "lived" — in both a good and bad sense — on 35th Street. In contrast, people living in the Lakeland community seem to be living in a bubble they are afraid will burst. Which setting seems more realistic and truthful? Discuss the differences and similarities that exist between 35th Street and Lakeland.

4   Thirty-fifth Street has always been a dumping ground for one kind of craziness or another, a place for people who don't fit in anywhere else. Why does it appeal to Tempestt?

5   What is ironic about the Nicholae plan (see p. 303)?

6   Why does Alfred Mayes confess to killing Valerie? Explain his role in her death. Who else could be held responsible for pushing her off the 12th floor?

7   Dreams repeatedly collide with reality in the course of the novel. How do the the dreams of Southern blacks collide with the reality of life in the North? How does the black community ensconced in Lakeland impact the dreams of the black community on 35th Street? Do dreams and reality ever come together in a positive way?

8   Talk about the ways in which the depths of misery can lead to startling beauty. Where do you see evidence of this in the story?

"Exceptionally powerful . . . written in language that's stringent and commanding." — *Boston Sunday Globe*

THE POINT
and other stories

Author: Charles D'Ambrosio

Publisher: Back Bay Books, 1995

Available in:
Quality paperback, 256 pages. $11.95
(ISBN 0-316-17144-1)

Genre: Fiction

Summary

In the award-winning title story, a young narrator, wise beyond his years, guides a drunk woman home and confronts the legacy of his father's suicide. *"American Bullfrog"* crystallizes teenage loneliness and confusion, and *"Her Real Name"* is an excursion into the mythic American West. Richly textured and packed with incident and insight, these seven stories summon up a world of lingering grief and restless hope — and deliver an extraordinary reading experience.

Recommended by: *Boston Sunday Globe*

"Exceptionally powerful ... written in language that's stringent and commanding."

Author Biography

Charles D'Ambrosio's stories have appeared in the *New Yorker,* the *Paris Review,* and *Story,* as well as in *Best American Short Stories* and the *Pushcart* anthology. He is a recipient of the Aga Khan Fiction Prize, a Henfield/*Transatlantic Review* Award, an NEA grant, and a James Michener Fellowship. He lives in Seattle.

Topics to Consider

1 The stories in this collection revolve around life — living it, avoiding it, learning from it — and death. Discuss life lessons as they are introduced in this collection. How do they unfold? What do we learn? What are some of the universal similarities that exist among the stories and among the protagonists?

2 In *"The Point,"* Kurt develops his theory of the 'black hole'. What is the importance of this theory as it relates to this story? Do 'black holes' exist in any of the other stories?

3 In *"Her Real Name,"* motion becomes important. Movement is seen as salvation (if they keep moving the woman will live). Discuss motion as it relates to this story.

4 What irony do you see in *"Her Real Name?"* Why does Jonesy take responsibility for a sick woman?

5 The adolescent boy in *"American Bullfrog,"* like so many characters in this collection, is experiencing an emotional disconnection from his family. What events conspire to enable the boy to reconnect with his father? Do you think his reconnection will last?

6 In *"Jacinta,"* mountains become a metaphor for that which is large and dangerous. How does Dorothy and Bill's situation fit this metaphor? What is the mountain in their life and how do they deal with it?

7 Does the model that Neal creates in *"All Aboard"* replace his real world? What is the effect of Flajole's death? Does it pull Neal into the real world or encourage his escape into his model world?

8 In *"Open House,"* Bobby refers to an experience as an echo within an echo. What does this mean to you?

9 How can the same activity — in this case, fishing — generate hopelessness in one individual and hope in another? Compare fishing in both *"Lyricism"* and *"Open House."*

10 Discuss the father figures in this collection of stories. Which "father" offers hope? Destruction? Connection?

RED EARTH
AND POURING RAIN

Author: Vikram Chandra

Publisher: Back Bay Books, 1995
(Little, Brown and Company)

Available in:
Hardcover, 542 pages. $24.95
(ISBN 0-316-13276-4)
Quality paperback, 560 pages. $14.95
(ISBN 0-316-13293-4)

Genre: Fiction

Summary

Chandra's novel is a contemporary *Thousand and One Nights*, with an eighteenth-century warrior-poet — now reincarnated as a typewriting monkey — and an Indian student home from college in America switching off as our Scheherazades. Ranging from bloody battles in colonial India to college anomie in California, from Hindu gods to MTV, from the pursuit of a legendary murderer in London to a cricket match in Houston, *Red Earth and Pouring Rain* is a remarkable meditation on quests and homecomings, good and evil, storytelling and redemption.

Recommended by: *Los Angeles Times Book Review*

"A magnificent tour de force: one of the finest Indian novels of the decade."

Author Biography

Born in New Delhi, India, in 1961, Vikram Chandra lives in India and America. He attended Pomona College in California and the Columbia University Film School and received an M.A. from Johns Hopkins University and an M.F.A. from the University of Houston. His stories have appeared in *The New Yorker* and *The Paris Review*. He can be reached by e-mail at vchandra@inter-ramp.com.

Topics to Consider

1   The Table of Contents is divided into five books: the Book of War and Ancestors, the Book of Learning and Desolation, the Book of Revenge and Madness, and the Book of the Return. Does a single theme integrate the stories within each book? What are the differences among the books? What relationship do the segments entitled *"What Really Happened"* bear to the other stories?

2   What does the book say about the power of story-telling? Is there any special story that has passed along within your family?

3   Stories often combine elements of past and present. Is one element more important than the other?

4   Both western and Indian viewpoints are represented in the book. Where is the clash between them most obvious? Does either emerge as most valid? Are the two perspectives mutually exclusive or can they co-exist?

5   In the story *"Janvi Defends Her Honour,"* it is said of the elephants that "they understand that it is better to endure and survive than to say no and die." Do you know anyone about whom you might say the same thing? Under what circumstances might one choose death over survival?

6   While working as a printer, Sanjay learns the "lesson of karma." Is this a lesson that westerners can understand?

7   At first, the monkey Sanjay tells stories in order to prolong his life. During the telling, does his purpose change?

8   If you had been a member of the audience, what effect, if any, would the stories have had on you?

9   The book tells of many journeys. Sometimes the journey is labeled a quest, sometimes an exile. What's the difference? What is everyone searching for?

RESISTANCE

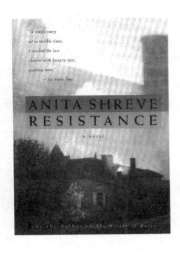

Author: Anita Shreve

Publisher: Back Bay Books, 1995
(Little, Brown and Company)

Available in:
Hardcover, 222 pages. $21.95
(ISBN 0-316-78999-2)
Quality paperback, 240 pages. $12.95
(ISBN 0-316-78984-4)

Genre: Fiction

Summary

In *Resistance,* Anita Shreve uses a wartime setting to sharpen the themes she has explored in previous novels — and leads us into a harrowing world where forbidden passions have catastrophic consequences. In a Nazi-occupied Belgian village, Claire Daussois, the wife of a resistance worker, shelters a wounded American bomber pilot in a secret attic hideaway. As she nurses him back to health, Claire falls in love, and is soon locked in a passionate affair that seems strong enough to conquer all — until the brute realities of war intrude, shattering every idea she ever had about love, trust, and betrayal.

Recommended by: *Publishers Weekly*

"Superb ... Explores themes of love and loss with piercing clarity."

Author Biography

Anita Shreve is the author of the acclaimed novels *Eden Close, Strange Fits of Passion,* and *Where or When.* Her award-winning short stories and nonfiction have appeared in the *New York Times Magazine, Cosmopolitan,* and *Esquire.*

Topics to Consider

1   The personal tragedy of Claire and Ted is inextricably connected with the larger story of the war. Discuss some of the other personal tragedies that are glimpsed in the story, and how tragedy can affect a relationship.

2   What do you think Claire's life would have been like if there had never been a war and she and Henri had lived out their lives in a peaceful Belgian village?

3   Just before Ted and Claire make love for the first time, Ted briefly wrestles with his conscience: "To touch Claire ... was to trespass against her husband and, indeed, against all the people who had conspired to try to save him." His next thought, however, is that the war has changed all the rules, and he reaches out for Claire in the attic room. How do you feel about his reasoning? What might you be thinking if you were Claire?

4   Does it seem reasonable to you that Claire would take such serious precautions for her own as well as her refugee's safety for so long, then risk a public appearance with Ted a few days before he is to leave? If so, why?

5   Consider the viewpoint that Henri, not Claire or Ted, is the most tragic character in the story. What elements support this view? Were your feelings about Henri any different at the end of the book?

6   While in the prison camps, Ted struggles with the thought that Claire may have been involved in betraying him to the Germans. Did he ever come to grips with his doubt before he died?

7   The story comes full circle at the end, when Ted's son and Claire meet and talk after the monument inauguration, and Tom meets his half-sister. What do you imagine Claire's life after the war to have been like? What about Ted?

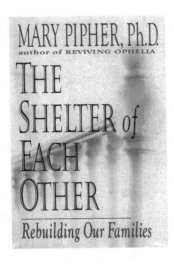

THE SHELTER OF EACH OTHER
Rebuilding Our Families

Author: Mary Pipher

Publisher: Grosset/Putnam, 1996

Available in:
Hardcover, 288 pages. $24.95
(ISBN 0-399-19331-6)

Genre: Nonfiction/Family Life

Summary

In *Reviving Ophelia,* psychologist Mary Pipher explored how our culture affects the mental health of teenage girls. In *The Shelter of Each Other,* Pipher turns her clear and empathic gaze on families. Families, she finds, have all the problems they've always had, plus many new ones created by psychology, media, and the avalanche of technology. The role of parents has changed dramatically in the last twenty years, and we are just beginning to grasp the implications of these changes. Pipher shows how parents can protect their families from what is dangerous, and how they can reconnect with the healing strength within all families.

Recommended by: *Kirkus Reviews*

"Lively, straightforward, and somewhat subversive. The Shelter of Each Other offers hope for the American family in a time that challenges its viability."

Author Biography

Dr. Mary Pipher is a psychologist in private practice. As a nationally touring lecturer, she has listened to stories about the cultural assault on families and what is being done, community by community, to save our most valuable institution. She lives in Lincoln, Nebraska.

Topics to Consider

1   How do you define family? What, if anything, do families do for their members that no one else can do?

2   Discuss the differences in childhood and in parenting between your era and today. What was better, or worse? How can we preserve the best of both eras for families?

3   How do we build a tiospaye, a sense of community, in our neighborhoods today? How can we help other people's children? What institutions can help us?

4   Is there a trade-off between privacy and lack of community? Is privacy sometimes a fancy word for isolation and fragmentation?

5   How do we balance the need to protect children with the need to raise them free of unnecessary fear?

6   How can we teach children to behave properly with one another? How can we help them make wise choices about their consumption, their use of tools and media, their friendships, their sexuality, and their time?

7   What useful work do we have for children in our community?

8   If we share the value that good adults do not do work that hurts children, how do we implement that value in a humane way?

9   What can we do to fight violent and sexualized media and the omnipresence of marketing to children?

10 What role has therapy played in the lives of families you know?

11 How do the tools you have change your family? What changes could you make in your family's use of television or computers that would increase family well-being?

12 Share family rituals and customs with one another. How can families celebrate themselves?

SNOW FALLING ON CEDARS

Author: David Guterson

Publisher: Vintage Books, 1995

Available in:
Quality paperback, 480 pages. $12.00
(ISBN 0-679-76402-X)

Genre: Fiction

Summary

San Piedro Island, north of Puget Sound, is a place so iso-lated that no one who lives there can afford to make enemies. But in 1954 a local fisherman is found suspiciously drowned, and a Japanese American named Kabuo Miyamoto is charged with his murder. In the course of the ensuing trial, it becomes clear that what is at stake is more than one man's guilt, as San Piedro is haunted by the mem-ory of what happened to its Japanese residents during World War II, when an entire community was sent into exile while its neighbors watched. This novel has been widely praised for its eloquent dramati-zation of themes of love, justice, racism, community, and conscience.

Recommended by: Pico Iyer, *Time*

" ... *A beautifully assured and full-bodied novel [that] becomes a tender examination of fairness and forgiveness* ..."

Author Biography

David Guterson received his M.A. from the University of Washington, where he studied under the writer Charles Johnson. It was there that he developed his ideas about the moral function of literature. After moving to Bainbridge Island, Guterson taught English at the local high school and began writing for *Sports Illustrated* and *Harper's*, where he is now a contributing editor. His books include ***The Country Ahead of Us, the Country Behind.*** ***Snow Falling on Cedars*** won the 1995 PEN/ Faulkner Award.

Topics to Consider

1 As we follow the trial, we are compelled to ask larger questions about the nature of truth, guilt, and responsibility. Which characters are aware that there is more at stake than one man's guilt?

2 What role does snow play — both literally and metaphorically — in the book? How does nature shape this novel?

3 There are places in the book where people are depersonalized — detached from their identities. What effect does depersonalization have upon our society?

4 Hatsue, as a teenager, rebels against her mother's values and at one point declares, "I don't want to be Japanese." How "normal" is her estrangement?

5 Compared to the *San Piedro Review,* what role does a newspaper play in the life and times of your community?

6 If you know someone affected by war, how does their experience compare to the ways in which the book's characters were affected?

7 How do Kabuo's and Hatsue's values determine their behavior, particularly their responses to internment, war, and imprisonment? How do their values clash with those of the Anglo community, even as they sometimes resemble them?

8 Racism is a persistent theme in this novel. In what ways do the book's Japanese characters respond to the hostility of their white neighbors?

9 Although almost all the novel's white characters are guilty of racism, only one of them — Etta Heine — emerges unsympathetically. How do her values and motives differ from those of the others?

10 What does the disparity between Hatsue's memories and Ishmael's suggest about the nature of love?

11 What is the significance of the novel's last sentence: "Accident ruled every corner of the universe except the chambers of the human heart"?

THE SOUL
OF THE NIGHT
An Astronomical Pilgrimage

Author: Chet Raymo

Publisher: Hungry Mind Press, 1996

Available in:
Quality paperback, 210 pages. $15.00
(ISBN 1-886913-11-0)

Genre: Science/Nature & Outdoors

Summary

Balanced between poetry and physics, astronomer Chet Raymo's elegant essays link the phenomena of the night sky with the human mind and spirit, as he ranges through the realms of mythology, literature, religion, and anthropology. The reader learns of black holes, galaxies, the Big Bang, the changing pattern of the universe and our place in it. Those interested in the relationship between science and faith will enjoy this book.

Recommended by: Krista Hunter, *Village Books,* Bellingham, WA

*"Chet Raymo has an enchanting gift, charming even the stars. I'm quite sure **The Soul of the Night** is a book even Henry Thoreau would have amply delighted in. Thank the heavens for this great and graceful book."*

Author Biography

Chet Raymo teaches physics and astronomy at Stonehill College in Massachusetts. For thirty-two years he has been a teacher, writer, illustrator and naturalist, exploring the relationships between science, nature, and the humanities. He has published eight books on science, including *365 Starry Nights* and *Honey from Stone.* His second novel, *The Dork of Cork,* became the motion picture "Frankie Starlight."

Topics to Consider

1   The subtitle of the book is "An Astronomical Pilgrimage." A pilgrimage is a journey to a sacred place or a seeking. What is the sacred place? What is sought?

2   In his introduction, the author speaks of those special transcendent moments when "the grandeur that abides in the night flares out (in the words of the poet Gerard Manley Hopkins) 'like shining from shook foil.'" What are some of these moments recounted in the book? How do we recognize such moments in our own lives?

3   In the first chapter of the book, the author speaks of silence, and specifically the silence of the night, as a source of meaning. In what different senses is the cosmos silent? How can silence be a source of meaning?

4   Darkness, silence: These are recurring themes throughout the book, as prerequisites for contemplation. In what ways does contemporary culture reinforce or undermine these values?

5   In many ways, the night sky would seem to be the most distant and indifferent element of our lives. In what ways does the author bring the night sky down to earth, or lift us into the stars?

6   Are there moral themes developed in the book? What are they? What is their relevance, if any, to our own lives?

7   We hear much today about the so-called conflict of science and religion. How does **The Soul of the Night** relate to this apparent antagonism? Would you call this book a work of science or a work of religion? Why?

8   The author quotes the naturalist John Burroughs: "To know is not all, it is only half. To love is the other half." How does this relate to the author's "pilgrimage"?

9   If you had to choose a single passage that summarizes the significance of the book *for you,* what would it be?

THE SPARROW

Author: Mary Doria Russell

Publisher: Villard, 1996

Available in:
Hardcover, 408 pages. $23.00
(ISBN 0-679-45150-1)

Genre: Fiction

Summary

The Sparrow is a novel about a remarkable man, a living saint, a life-long celibate and Jesuit priest, Emilio Sandoz, who undergoes an experience so harrowing and profound that it makes him question the existence of God. This experience — the first contact between human beings and intelligent extraterrestrial life — begins with a small mistake and ends in catastrophe. Sandoz is the only surviving member of a crew that went to discover a new planet. Like other great explorers of the New World, they were confronted by a civilization so alien and incomprehensible that they were individually compelled to wonder at what it means to be human. On his return, Sandoz must face a Jesuit inquiry and public condemnation as he is accused of the most heinous of crimes. *The Sparrow* is a tale of spirituality, cynicism, and ultimately faith in our complex world.

Recommended by: Colleen McCullough

"... a startling, engrossing and moral work of fiction."

Author Biography

Mary Doria Russell is a paleo-anthropologist with specialties in bone biology and biomechanics who has done extensive field work in Australia and Croatia. After quitting academia and writing computer manuals, she began work on *The Sparrow*. She lives in Cleveland, Ohio with her husband Don and their son Daniel, and is currently working on a sequel titled *Children of God*.

Topics to Consider

1   This story is set in the years 2014-2060. Does futuristic literature require anything special of the reader?

2   The Jesuit mission to Rakhat was undertaken "for the greater glory of God. They meant no harm." Was the conduct of the mission consistent with this goal? Where and why did the mission go wrong? Was any of the outcome preventable?

3   It is asserted in the book that the Jesuits espouse the philosophy that the end justifies the means, "doing what seemed necessary in the service of God, for the good of souls." Is the mission conducted in this spirit? Are the hearings? Is this philosophy supported by the experiences depicted in the book?

4   The members of the mission constitute a small community living in close quarters. How do they adapt to the challenges and rewards of such a situation? How do you think you would do in similar circumstances?

5   During the hearings conducted after Emilio Sandoz returns to earth, what is accomplished? How are any participants changed by their encounter?

6   Do the characters find God? Of what significance — if any — is the fact that the original celestial music turns out to have been pornography, not prayer?

7   What do the characters learn about love, spirituality, commitment, dedication, and purpose?

8   Is the Jesuit mission to Rakhat scientific or religious? What does the planetary journey represent to the individuals involved and to the world? Why do the Jesuits plan to send another group?

9   Is the book an expression of faith or of doubt?

TO DESTROY YOU IS NO LOSS
The Odyssey of a Cambodian Family

Author: JoAn Dewey Criddle

Publisher: East/West Bridge, 1996

Available in:
Quality paperback, 294 pages, photos.
$16.95 (ISBN 0-9632205-1-9)

Genre: Biography/Oral History/
Asian-American

Summary

Often called "The Cambodian *Diary of Anne Frank*," this award-winning book follows one prominent Cambodian family's struggles to survive four years of unprecedented brutality and wanton destruction during Pol Pot's communist Khmer Rouge regime. Featuring fifteen-year-old Teeda, it is the true story of the four generation Butt family's efforts to stay alive, and their eventual terror-filled escape attempts from a war-ravaged, famine-riddled nation. Catapulted into a four-year-long nightmare of hard labor, brutality, and constant fear of detection and death, this family exhibits the tenacity of the human will to survive.

Recommended by: *Providence Sunday Journal*

"... Like the finest examples of Holocaust literature, it is an affirmation of the human spirit, of the will to prevail ... an extraordinary book ... about the still unresolved tragedy of the world's refugees."

Author Biography

JoAn D. Criddle helped sponsor Teeda to America. Her second book about Teeda's family is *Bamboo & Butterflies: From Refugee to Citizen.* Criddle's writing niche is first-person biographies of exemplary, but little-known minority Americans. Her books are both authoritative and highly readable. An enthusiastic wife, mother, grandmother, and minority advocate, lecturer, and consultant, Criddle travels world-wide but makes her home in California.

Topics to Consider

1 Did you identify with any member(s) of Teeda's family? If so, who and why? How might the account differ had the story been told by a family member other than Teeda?

2 What insights can you apply to interactions with other Southeast Asian-Americans or even refugees and immigrants from other parts of the world?

3 Many people report that they read this book in one sitting, that it was an emotional roller coaster ride for them. Describe your emotional response to this story and to the members of Teeda's family. Were there places in the narration where you felt anger, frustration, sorrow, joy, hopelessness, helplessness, fury, delight?

4 How did this book add to your knowledge of Cambodia's geography, history, and/or culture? Your understanding of the role Cambodia played in the Vietnam war?

5 Discuss the obligation America and other western nations might have in offering refugees a safe haven.

6 In what ways is this account of a young Cambodian woman in the 1970s reminiscent of Anne Frank's experiences in Nazi Germany?

7 Were the extreme left-leaning Khmer Rouge and the ultra-right wing Nazi leaders aberrations, or is there a typical pattern that tyrants use irrespective of their political philosophies? In what other times and places in the world have similar 'solutions' been found for 'undesirables'? What can be done to stop today's tyrants and to anticipate tomorrow's would-be tyrants?

8 Conditions must change and safety nets established before the world's refugee problems can be adequately addressed. What course of action do you suggest for the United Nations? For first-world countries? For our government? For organizations and individuals in this country and abroad? What can you and your circle of friends do?

TREE OF HEAVEN

Author: R.C. Binstock

Publisher: Soho Press, 1995

Available in:
Hardcover, 224 pages. $22.00
(ISBN 1-56947-038-3)
Quality paperback, 224 pages. $12.00
(ISBN 1-56947-069-3)

Genre: Fiction

Summary

Tree of Heaven is set in China in 1938. After the surrender of a Chinese Army, the city of Nanking had been left defenseless and at the mercy of the Japanese Army. The ensuing slaughter and rape of the civilian population has just taken place. Kuroda, a Japanese junior officer, an educated man trained as a botanist, finds himself left behind by the army, in charge of a garrison town northeast of the city. He rescues Li, a starving, filthy Chinese refugee and makes her his servant. In their isolation, a relationship grows between these very disparate individuals. Captor and captive become intimate earning Li the enmity of the Chinese villagers and Kuroda the scorn of his men. Told in alternating voices, the story of their doomed affair is a compelling exploration of love, obsession and loss.

Recommended by: *Newsday*

"A compelling meditation on the use and abuse of power ...a triumph of unobtrusive historical research and imaginative empathy."

Author Biography

R.C. Binstock is a graduate of Harvard College. He lives in Cambridge, Massachusetts with his wife and daughters. He has also written *The Light of Home,* a story collection published in 1992, and *The Soldier.* He considers *Tree of Heaven* a novel of "the other holocaust" — atrocities committed in Asia no less tragic because they have been hidden from most Americans.

Topics to Consider

1   Given the political situation in China at the time, was Japanese control preferable to civil war?

2   The Japanese and the Chinese each regarded the other as culturally and "racially" inferior. What were the characteristics each attributed to the other? Is there truth to stereotypes of any kind?

3   What was the status of women in China in 1938? What would you expect it to be like today? How can cultural attitudes influence the development of a relationship? How were Li and Kuroda affected?

4   Kuroda says he fears his men more than the enemy. Why? What does this say about Japanese society? About Kuroda's feelings of guilt and shame?

5   Does having an "exalted" leader – like Emperor Hirohito – make it easier to follow orders without questioning them?

6   Is it a valid defense to claim that you "were only following orders"? What other choice could a soldier make?

7   Is Kuroda's rescue of Li an unselfish act? Is it heroic? How does her presence punish Kuroda? How does it reward him? Is Li really a slave?

8   Was Li's offer to sleep with Kuroda, her captor, made freely? Is this intimacy, born of circumstance, based on mutual affection or a choice made purely for survival? Does she love him? Is she guilty of treason?

9   Does Kuroda really love Li? Does he really love his wife? What does each woman represent to him? Is he guilty of treason?

10 Why does Li leave after Kuroda's death? Why does she turn back? Why does she tear open her tunic and offer herself to the soldiers?

11 What is the symbolism of the tree of heaven?

THE WEB OF LIFE
Weaving The Values That Sustain Us

Author: Richard Louv

Publisher: Conari, 1996

Available in:
Hardcover, 250 pages. $14.95
(ISBN 1-57324-036-2)

Genre: Inspiration/Current Events

Summary

Through eloquent stories, poignant discussion, and a collection of quotes, Richard Louv explores the web of life that connects people and the strands that make it up: family, community, love, spirit, purpose, nature, childhood, adulthood, and humanity. Louv makes a compelling case that our future depends on rebuilding this fragile web of life through strengthening and treasuring our friendships, our business relationships, and our families. He reveals the small moments of our lives, shining the light of love upon them and illuminating their greatness.

Recommended by: J. Douglas Bates

"Louv writes about values with more heart, more wisdom than any other author ... in the country."

Author Biography

Award-winning journalist and author **Richard Louv** is a columnist for *The San Diego Union-Tribune* and a contributing editor to *Parent's Magazine*. His ground-breaking books include ***Childhood's Future*** (the subject of a Bill Moyers PBS special), ***Fatherlove, 101 Things You Can Do For Your Children's Future,*** and ***America II.*** In his columns, Louv writes about family issues, the environment, technology, cities, immigration, personal and public ethics, grass-roots politics, and renewal in American life.

Topics to Consider

1   Do you feel connected — part of something bigger than yourself? What form does your web take?

2   Discuss the strands of your life and the web you weave. Which strands are weak and which are strong? Why?

3   How can we better acknowledge the small strands that make up the web of our family lives, and how can we better preserve our family memories? How are you and your family preserving your stories?

4   Who are the significant people in your life that have made you feel connected — to nature, to community, to spirituality?

5   How can we better connect our children to nature?

6   Can computers and the Internet help us weave the strands of family and community?

7   How can we be "good parent-neighbors"?

8   Where are your "great good places," the places you hang out, connect with friends, meet people you don't know? How do these places shape you?

9   What are the more difficult aspects of community? Do you have "skinwalkers" in your life?

10 Where is your "one true place," a spot in the universe where you belong?

11 Who was your first love?

12 What do our pets teach us?

13 What memories sustain us, and how can our memories heal us?

¡YO!

Author: Julia Alvarez

Publisher: Algonquin Books, 1997

Available in:
Hardcover, pages. $18.95
(ISBN 1-56512-157-0)

Genre: Fiction

Summary

¡Yo! is a novel about what happens when an author really does "write what she knows." Obsessed by human stories, Latina novelist Yolanda García has managed to put herself at the center of many lives. Thrice married, she's also managed to remain childless while giving very public "birth" to her highly autobiographical writing. She's famous for it. Now her "characters" want a chance to tell their side of it. Everybody who's ever been caught in Yo's web — from her sisters to her third husband — can hardly wait to talk. The stories they tell on celebrated writer Yolanda García (known to her intimates as "Yo") deliver delicious insight into the very nature of artistic creation and the material from which it is built.

Recommended by: *Publishers Weekly*

" ... a triumph of imaginative virtuosity ... an entrancing novel ... "

Author Biography

Julia Alvarez is the author of two previous award-winning novels, *How the Garcia Girls Lost Their Accents,* and *In the Time of the Butterflies.* She has also published three highly acclaimed books of poetry. Her essays, stories, and poems have appeared in many magazines, including *The New York Times Magazine,* and *USA Weekend.* She lives with her husband in Vermont and teaches at Middlebury College.

Topics to Consider

1 "Yo," as well as a nickname, is the first person singular pronoun, *I*, in Spanish, yet Yolanda herself never has the opportunity to use the personal pronoun. Why doesn't Yo ever have a chance to speak for herself?

2 From time to time, Yolanda makes a big deal about being Latina. How important is her ethnicity to her sense of herself as a person and writer?

3 What is the significance of each of the literary terms in the titles of the sixteen narratives? Why do you think the author chose to include them?

4 Yo claims that men don't understand her bicultural self, that they prevent her from being a writer. Do you agree? How well does Alvarez present the points of view of male characters?

5 Why do you think Yolanda, unlike her sisters, has never had children?

6 The various images of womanhood Yolanda García embodies in the minds of her various biographers range from aggressive competitor to sexy glamour puss to frightened prey. How would *you* characterize her? Which of the story-tellers sees Yo most clearly as she really is?

7 Yo is accused of many transgressions in her pursuit of a writing career — from her sisters who claim that she has exposed their personal lives to the public eye to her former student who believes she has plagiarized his work. What do these accusations say about where a writer's real life stops and her fiction begins?

8 Julia Alvarez has defined "truth" as "all the points around the circle" and plot as "a quilt, which is a way that I think a lot of women experience plot, as opposed to the hero directed on his adventure ... against all odds, doing what her needs to do." How does the form of this character novel illustrate her image of plot direction as "relational" as opposed to "directional"?

9 How do the various portraits of Yolanda and their different layers of meaning add to one another? How do they build to a crescendo in her father's narrative?

RESOURCES

Newsletters

Reverberations News Journal, Rachel Jacobsohn's publication of the Association of Book Group Readers and Leaders. Annual membership including subscription is $18. Contact: ABGRL, Box 885, Highland Park, IL 60035, (847) 266-0431.

Booknews and Views, quarterly newsletter of Books, Etcetera. Annual subscription is $10. Contact: Books, Etcetera, 228 Commercial Street #1957, Nevada City, CA 95959, (916) 478-9400.

Literary Trips

FPT Special Interest Tours. Annual trips abroad with Diana Altman, Women's National Book Association member and travel consultant. May 23-31, 1997, A Literary Tour of Ireland. Contact: FPT, 186 Alewife Brook Parkway, Cambridge, MA 02138, phone (800) 645-0001, fax (617) 661-3354, or e-mail dma@fpt.com.

Literary Getaways to Northern California with Judith Palarz. Book discussions and sightseeing for lovers of literature. Two days, two nights at a Bed & Breakfast Inn in Nevada City, the Napa Valley or Half Moon Bay. Contact: Books, Etcetera, 228 Commercial Street #1957, Nevada City, CA 95959, (916) 478-9400.

Books

Minnesota Women's Press Great Books.
Contact: Minnesota Women's Press, 771 Raymond Avenue, Saint Paul, MN 55114, (612) 646-3968.

The Reading Group Handbook by Rachel W. Jacobsohn.
Published by Hyperion, ISBN 0-7868-8002-3, $10.95

The New York Public Library Guide to Reading Groups
by Rollene Saal. Published by Crown, ISBN 0-517-88357-0, $11.

What to Read: The Essential Guide for Reading Group Members and Other Book Lovers by Mickey Pearlman.
Published by Harper Perennial, ISBN 0-06-095061-7, $9.

The Book Group Book: A Thoughtful Guide to Forming and Enjoying a Stimulating Book Discussion Group by Ellen Slezak.
Published by Chicago Review Press, ISBN 1-55652-195-2, $9.95

INDEX BY AUTHOR

INDEX BY AUTHOR

(continued)

INDEX BY AUTHOR

(continued)

INDEX BY GENRE

Non-Fiction

INDEX BY GENRE

Fiction

INDEX BY GENRE

Fiction (continued)

INDEX BY TOPIC

BOOK GROUP MEMBERS

Name _____
    Day phone _____ Eve. phone _____

Name _____
    Day phone _____ Eve. phone _____

Name _____
    Day phone _____ Eve. phone _____

Name _____
    Day phone _____ Eve. phone _____

Name _____
    Day phone _____ Eve. phone _____

Name _____
    Day phone _____ Eve. phone _____

Name _____
    Day phone _____ Eve. phone _____

Name _____
    Day phone _____ Eve. phone _____

Name _____
    Day phone _____ Eve. phone _____

Name _____
    Day phone _____ Eve. phone _____

Name _____
    Day phone _____ Eve. phone _____

BOOK GROUP MEETING DATES

January   _____

February   _____

March   _____

April   _____

May   _____

June   _____

July   _____

August   _____

September _____

October   _____

November   _____

December   _____

January   _____

February   _____

March   _____

1997

January 1997

S	M	T	W	T	F	S
			1	2	3	4
5	6	7	8	9	10	11
12	13	14	15	16	17	18
19	20	21	22	23	24	25
26	27	28	29	30	31	

February 1997

S	M	T	W	T	F	S
						1
2	3	4	5	6	7	8
9	10	11	12	13	14	15
16	17	18	19	20	21	22
23	24	25	26	27	28	

March 1997

S	M	T	W	T	F	S
						1
2	3	4	5	6	7	8
9	10	11	12	13	14	15
16	17	18	19	20	21	22
23/30	24/31	25	26	27	28	29

April 1997

S	M	T	W	T	F	S
		1	2	3	4	5
6	7	8	9	10	11	12
13	14	15	16	17	18	19
20	21	22	23	24	25	26
27	28	29	30			

May 1997

S	M	T	W	T	F	S
				1	2	3
4	5	6	7	8	9	10
11	12	13	14	15	16	17
18	19	20	21	22	23	24
25	26	27	28	29	30	31

June 1997

S	M	T	W	T	F	S
1	2	3	4	5	6	7
8	9	10	11	12	13	14
15	16	17	18	19	20	21
22	23	24	25	26	27	28
29	30					

July 1997

S	M	T	W	T	F	S
		1	2	3	4	5
6	7	8	9	10	11	12
13	14	15	16	17	18	19
20	21	22	23	24	25	26
27	28	29	30	31		

August 1997

S	M	T	W	T	F	S
					1	2
3	4	5	6	7	8	9
10	11	12	13	14	15	16
17	18	19	20	21	22	23
24/31	25	26	27	28	29	30

September 1997

S	M	T	W	T	F	S
	1	2	3	4	5	6
7	8	9	10	11	12	13
14	15	16	17	18	19	20
21	22	23	24	25	26	27
28	29	30				

October 1997

S	M	T	W	T	F	S
			1	2	3	4
5	6	7	8	9	10	11
12	13	14	15	16	17	18
19	20	21	22	23	24	25
26	27	28	29	30	31	

November 1997

S	M	T	W	T	F	S
						1
2	3	4	5	6	7	8
9	10	11	12	13	14	15
16	17	18	19	20	21	22
23/30	24	25	26	27	28	29

December 1997

S	M	T	W	T	F	S
	1	2	3	4	5	6
7	8	9	10	11	12	13
14	15	16	17	18	19	20
21	22	23	24	25	26	27
28	29	30	31			

NOTES

NOTES

NOTES

About Paz & Associates

This publication was developed and produced by Paz & Associates, whose mission is to join with publishers and bookstores to develop resources and skills that promote books and reading. We offer a variety of products and services to bookstores, publishers, and other book-related organizations, including the following:

- consulting on marketing, human resources, store design, merchandising, and business operations
- the monthly newsletter *Independent Bookselling Today!*
- *Opening a Bookstore: The Essential Planning Guide*
- *The Training Guide to FrontLine Bookselling*
- *Exceptional FrontLine Bookselling: It's All About Service,* a 60 minute training video

For additional copies of this publication, please call your local bookstore or contact us at the address and phone number below. We will be happy to let you know of a bookstore in your area that has obtained copies of *Reading Group Choices*. Quantities are limited.

Paz & Associates
2106 Twentieth Avenue South
Nashville, TN 37212-4312

800/260-8605 — phone
615/298-9864 — fax
dpaz@pazbookbiz.com — email

Women's National Book Association

WNBA is an organization that brings together women and men who value the written word. There are ten chapters located in Atlanta, Binghamton, Boston, Dallas, Detroit, Los Angeles, Nashville, New York, San Francisco, and Washington D.C. To find out how to contact a chapter near you, or to learn how to start a new chapter, write or call:

WNBA
160 Fifth Avenue
New York, NY 10010
212/675-7805